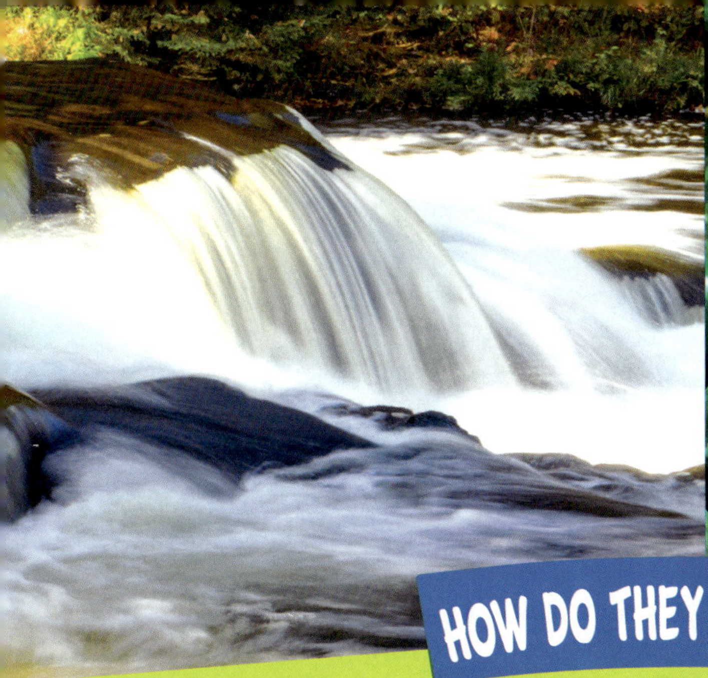

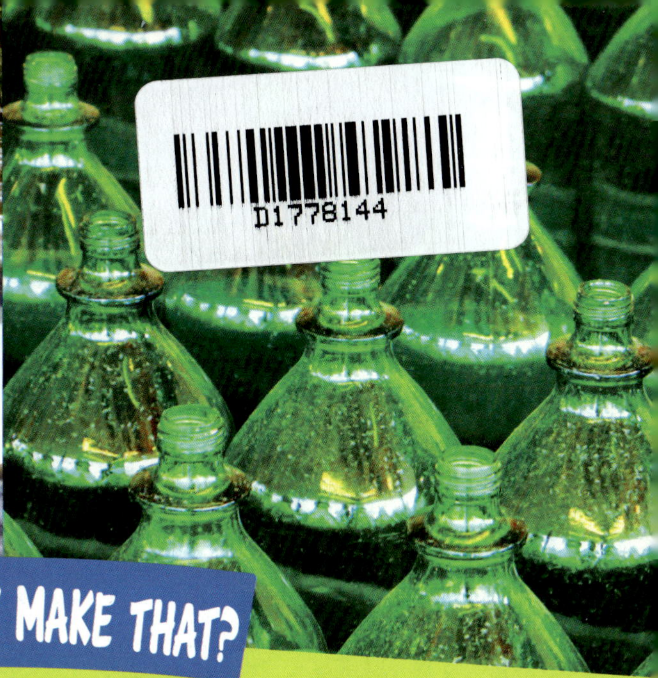

HOW DO THEY MAKE THAT?

SODA POP

Rachel Lynette and John Willis

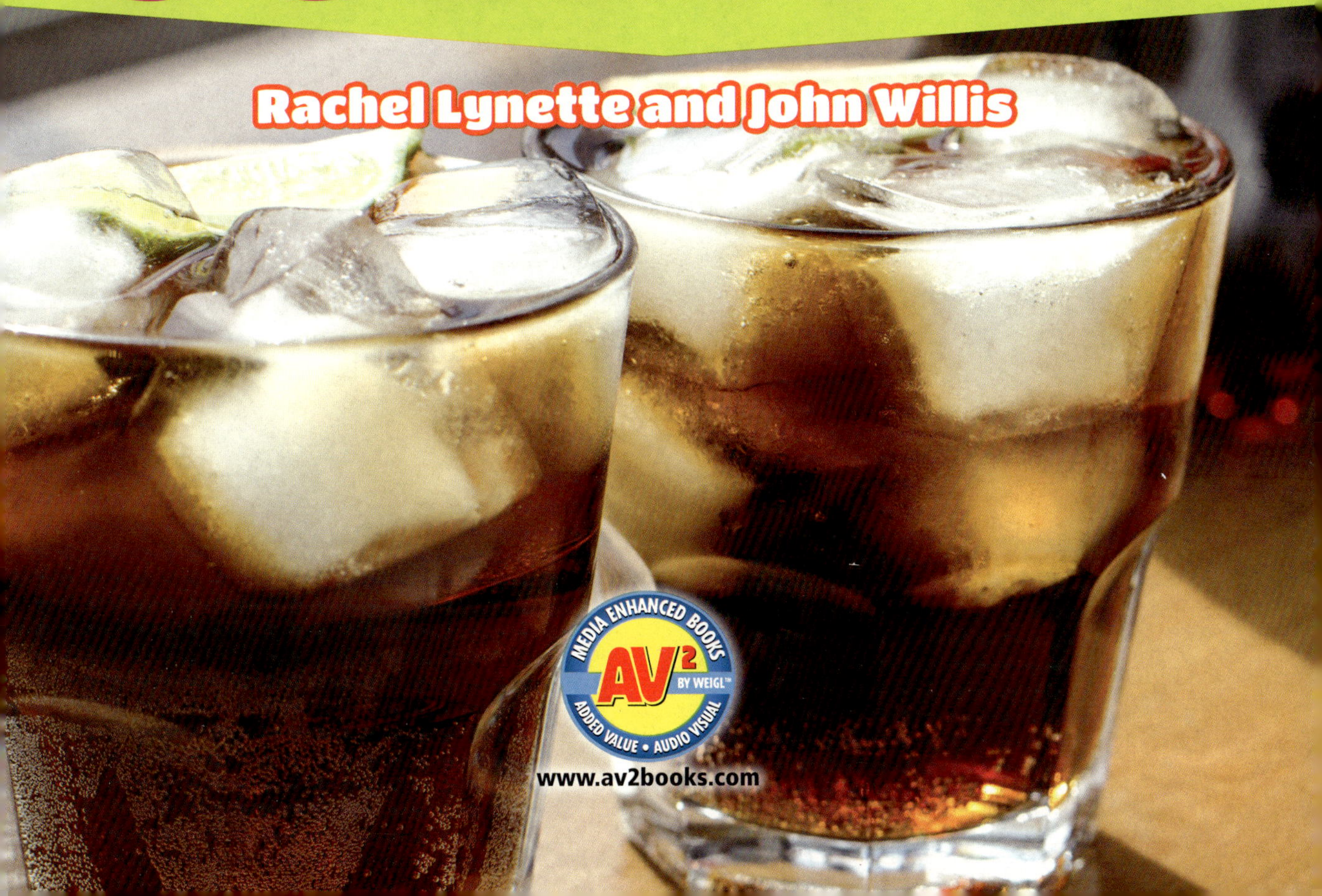

MEDIA ENHANCED BOOKS
AV2 BY WEIGL
ADDED VALUE • AUDIO VISUAL
www.av2books.com

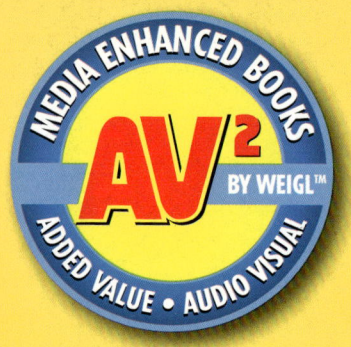

AV² provides enriched content that supplements and complements this book. Weigl's AV² books strive to create inspired learning and engage young minds in a total learning experience.

Your AV² Media Enhanced books come alive with...

 **Audio** Listen to sections of the book read aloud.

 **Key Words** Study vocabulary, and complete a matching word activity.

 **Video** Watch informative video clips.

 **Quizzes** Test your knowledge.

 **Embedded Weblinks** Gain additional information for research.

 **Slide Show** View images and captions, and prepare a presentation.

 **Try This!** Complete activities and hands-on experiments.

Go to www.av2books.com, and enter this book's unique code.

BOOK CODE

J964886

AV² by Weigl brings you media enhanced books that support active learning.

... and much, much more!

Published by AV² by Weigl
350 5th Avenue, 59th Floor
New York, NY 10118
Website: www.av2books.com

Copyright © 2017 AV² by Weigl
All rights reserved. No part of this publication may be reproduced, stored in a retrieval system, or transmitted in any form or by any means, electronic, mechanical, photocopying, recording, or otherwise, without the prior written permission of the publisher.

Library of Congress Cataloging-in-Publication Data

Names: Lynette, Rachel, author | and Willis, John, author.
Title: Soda pop / Rachel Lynette.
Description: New York, NY : AV2 by Weigl, [2017] | Series: How do they make that? | Includes bibliographical references and index.
Identifiers: LCCN 2016005664 (print) | LCCN 2016006700 (ebook) | ISBN 9781489645432 (hard cover : alk. paper) | ISBN 9781489650047 (soft cover : alk. paper) | ISBN 9781489645449 (Multi-user ebk.)
Subjects: LCSH: Carbonated beverages--Juvenile literature. | Soft drinks--Juvenile literature. | Carbonated beverage industry--Juvenile literature.
Classification: LCC TP630 .L96 2017 (print) | LCC TP630 (ebook) | DDC 663--dc23
LC record available at http://lccn.loc.gov/2016005664

Printed in the United States of America in Brainerd, Minnesota
1 2 3 4 5 6 7 8 9 0 20 19 18 17 16

072016
210716

Project Coordinator: John Willis   Art Director: Terry Paulhus

Every reasonable effort has been made to trace ownership and to obtain permission to reprint copyright material. The publishers would be pleased to have any errors or omissions brought to their attention so that they may be corrected in subsequent printings.

Weigl acknowledges Getty Images, Dreamstime, Alamy, Newscom, Shutterstock, and iStock as its primary image suppliers for this title.

Contents

AV² Book Code 2
All Kinds of Soda Pop 4
At the Soda Pop Factory 6
Soda Pop Syrup 8
Fizz It 16
Into Bottles and Cans 20
Labels and Packing 24
Into Your Cup 28
Quiz 30
Key Words/Index 31
Log on to www.av2books.com 32

All Kinds of Soda Pop

There are all kinds of soda pop. Root beer, cola, and ginger ale are just a few. How many can you name? Soda pop is sold all over the world. It comes in bottles and cans. It also comes from a soda fountain at a restaurant or store.

What makes soda pop different from other drinks? Unlike juice or milk, soda pop is **carbonated**. That means it is full of tiny bubbles. Soda pop is almost always sweet and contains some kind of flavoring.

Have you thought about how soda pop is made? There are many steps. The first starts with water. Soda pop is mostly made from water. That water needs to be very clean.

The first carbonated drinks became popular in the 1840s.

The water in soda pop is much cleaner than water in nature.

At the Soda Pop Factory

If the water used to make soda is not clean, it will not taste right or have the right color. The water is cleaned in stages.

First, tiny bits of plants, animal matter, or minerals are taken out of the water. A certain gel is added to the water. The gel acts like a kind of glue. The tiny bits stick to it. They form a large glob called floc. Floc is caught as the water goes through sand and gravel filters. Filters allow liquid to pass through. Solids stick to the filters.

Next, all **bacteria** is taken out of the water. Most bacteria is harmless, but some kinds can make you sick. The water is poured into a large tank. Some **chlorine** is added. It takes about two hours for the chlorine to kill the bacteria. Then, the water is run through another filter. It takes out all of the chlorine. Now the water is ready to be made into soda pop.

Soda Pop Syrup

What makes soda pop taste so good? That sweet taste comes from the syrup. Each kind of soda pop uses a different syrup recipe. Soda pop syrup recipes are top-secret. Only a few people who work at a soda pop company know the secret recipes.

If you look at a can of soda pop, one of the first **ingredients** is sugar. Sometimes sugar has other names. Glucose, high fructose corn syrup, and sucrose are all names for different kinds of sugars.

There are about nine teaspoons of sugar in a 12 ounce (355 milliliter) can of cola.

The most common sweetener in soda is high fructose corn syrup.

Soda Pop 9

The syrup in soda pop is made mostly from sugar. The sugar comes from sugar beets, corn, or sugar cane. For diet drinks, an artificial sweetener is used. These include aspartame and saccharin. Unlike regular sugar, they do not make people gain weight.

The sugar used in soda pop comes to the factory as a liquid. It ships by tanker truck or train. This liquid sugar is mixed with other ingredients in a vat at the factory. These ingredients give soda pop its flavor and color.

Sweeteners and flavoring are mixed into syrup in large dosing stations.

Soda Pop 11

Some ingredients are natural, such as kola nut **extract** for cola-flavored soda and ginger for ginger ale. Small amounts of natural spices and oils from different plants are used in soda pop. Citric acid is also added to many kinds of soda pop. It gives the soda a slightly tart taste.

Many kinds of soda pop contain artificial flavorings. They are made from **chemicals**. These flavorings are less expensive than natural flavors. The artificial flavors also make the soda smell good. This makes people want to drink the soda pop even more.

Caffeine is also in many kinds of soda pop. Caffeine gives people a little extra energy and makes the soda taste better.

Citric acid comes from fruit.

Soda Pop 13

Other ingredients make soda pop look cloudy instead of clear or make it foamy. That is why root beer and ginger ale foam more than most kinds of soda pop. **Preservatives** keep the soda pop from going bad over time.

Once the syrup is mixed, it must be cleaned to remove bacteria. **Ultraviolet** light kills the bacteria. It is shone into the tank that holds the syrup. The light destroys some of the chemicals the bacteria need to live. Another way to kill the bacteria is to heat and cool the syrup quickly. This is called **pasteurization**.

Syrups made with fruit, such as lime or orange, must be pasteurized.

Water is added to the syrup in a large machine called a proportioner.

Fizz It

Now, it is time to add syrup to the water. A machine lets out the right amount into the water. The water and syrup are blended together in a special tank. Have you ever tasted soda pop that is flat? It has lost all of its fizz. That is what the soda pop would taste like at this point. The soda pop is all done. It just needs the bubbles.

Carbon dioxide was first added to water in 1767.

18   How Do They Make That?

The bubbles in soda pop come from a gas called **carbon dioxide**. Carbon dioxide has no taste, color, or smell. A machine adds carbon dioxide to the soda pop. This is done in a large tank called a carbonator. The amount of carbon dioxide that is added depends on the kind of soda pop in the tank. Fruit-flavored soda pop has less carbon dioxide than other kinds of soda pop. Colas have more carbon dioxide.

Into Bottles and Cans

Now it is time for the soda pop to be put into bottles or cans. Most soda pop is sold in plastic bottles rather than glass. Some bottles have a single serving. The larger 2 liter (a little more than 0.5 gallon) bottles are enough for several people. Most cans have only one serving.

The bottles or cans come from a different factory. All bottles must be washed, even ones that are brand new. They need to be very clean before they are loaded into the filling machine.

PepsiCo introduced the first plastic 2 liter bottle in 1970.

Soda Pop 21

Bottles travel to the filling machine on a **conveyor belt**. The filling machine carries the bottles around in a circle. The machine sucks all the air out of each bottle. Then, a spout is put into the top and the bottle is filled with soda pop. The bottle is full after it has gone the whole way around the circle. The process is similar for filling cans.

The spout comes out and the bottle goes to the capping machine. The bottles travel in a circle around the machine. It screws a plastic lid tightly onto the top of each bottle. Glass bottles may have metal lids rather than plastic ones. The metal lids are crimped on the sides to keep them on the bottles. For cans, a machine attaches the pull-tab cover.

Some bottling plants use recycled glass bottles instead of plastic.

Once a soda bottle is full, it is immediately capped to prevent air from getting in.

Soda pop bottle labels are usually made out of thin plastic film.

Labels and Packing

The plastic bottles still need their labels. The bottles and the soda pop cool as they move through the factory. If a label is stuck onto a cold bottle, the label could be ruined. It would get wet and not stick. **Water vapor** is in the air. It collects as tiny water drops on cold objects. To make labels stick, the bottles are warmed. They are sprayed with warm water and then dried with warm air. It is a bit like a car wash for bottles.

A machine puts glue on the backs of the labels. Then, it sticks the labels to the bottles. Both sides of the bottle are brushed by the machine.

More than 80 billion soda cans are used every year in the United States.

26   How Do They Make That?

This smooths the label down on the sides to make sure it will not peel off. Cans and glass bottles do not need labels. Information is printed right on the cans and bottles.

Soda cans, small plastic bottles, and glass bottles are put into different kinds of packages. They come in four-packs, six-packs, ten-packs, and larger packs. Large plastic bottles are sold alone. Each different soda package is packed into larger boxes. Now they are ready to ship.

People drink more soda pop in the United States than in any other country. Drinking too much soda is bad for you, though. It can cause people to gain too much weight. This can lead to many health problems.

Into Your Cup

The bottles and cans travel by truck and by train to stores where you can buy them. Some go to supermarkets or other stores. Other bottles and cans end up in **vending machines**. Not all soda pop comes from a can or a bottle. Soda pop also comes from a soda fountain. The soda fountain machines blend soda pop syrup with water and carbon dioxide. You just push a button and soda pop comes out of the spout and into your cup.

What flavor of soda pop do you like best? Have you ever mixed two or three flavors together? If you add vanilla ice cream to root beer, you can make a root beer float. Yum. Enjoy some soda pop for a special treat.

Soda pop can be bought almost anywhere and is fun to drink at a picnic or party.

Soda Pop 29

Quiz

Match the steps with the pictures.

A. Clean water
B. Make syrup
C. Mix syrup and water
D. Fill bottles
E. Cap bottles
F. At the store

Answers: 1.B 2.D 3.E 4.A 5.F 6.C

Key Words

bacteria: small living things that are harmful or helpful

caffeine: a chemical that is used in some kinds of soda pop and gives a person energy

carbon dioxide: a type of gas that has no smell or taste

carbonated: A drink that has carbon dioxide in it

chemicals: substances made using chemistry

chlorine: a gas that is added to water to kill germs and keep water clean

conveyor belt: a moving belt that takes materials from one place to another in a factory

extract: an ingredient with water taken out, which makes it very strong

ingredients: things that are added to a mixture, like items in a recipe list

pasteurization: when food is heated to a high temperature to kill harmful bacteria

preservatives: chemicals added to foods and drinks to keep them from spoiling

ultraviolet: light that cannot be seen with a person's eye

vending machine: a machine that you insert money into and food or drinks come out

water vapor: water in the air that cannot be seen.

Index

bacteria 7, 14
bottles 4, 20, 21, 22, 23, 24, 25, 27, 28, 30
caffeine 12
carbonated 4, 5
carbonator 19

chlorine 7

flavoring 4, 11, 12
floc 7

ingredients 8, 10, 12, 14

labels 24, 25, 27

pasteurization 14, 15
preservatives 14
soda fountain 4, 28
sugar 8, 10

syrup 8, 9, 10, 11, 14, 1, 16, 17, 28, 30

water 4, 6, 7, 16, 17, 18, 25, 28, 30

Log on to www.av2books.com

AV² by Weigl brings you media enhanced books that support active learning. Go to www.av2books.com, and enter the special code found on page 2 of this book. You will gain access to enriched and enhanced content that supplements and complements this book. Content includes video, audio, weblinks, quizzes, a slide show, and activities.

AV² Online Navigation

Audio
Listen to sections of the book read aloud.

Book Pages
AV² pages directly correspond to pages in the book.

Video
Watch informative video clips.

Embedded Weblinks
Gain additional information for research.

Key Words
Study vocabulary, and complete a matching word activity.

Try This!
Complete activities and hands-on experiments.

Quizzes
Test your knowledge.

Slide Show
View images and captions, and prepare a presentation.

AV² was built to bridge the gap between print and digital. We encourage you to tell us what you like and what you want to see in the future.

Sign up to be an AV² Ambassador at www.av2books.com/ambassador.

Due to the dynamic nature of the Internet, some of the URLs and activities provided as part of AV² by Weigl may have changed or ceased to exist. AV² by Weigl accepts no responsibility for any such changes. All media enhanced books are regularly monitored to update addresses and sites in a timely manner. Contact AV² by Weigl at 1-866-649-3445 or av2books@weigl.com with any questions, comments, or feedback.